STAY PROFITABLE IN AI MARKETING

BY

HENRY E. PARKINS

COPYRIGHT PAGE

TABLE OF CONTENTS

3

INTRODUCTION

In the dynamic realm of modern marketing, staying relevant and profitable requires not only adaptability but a keen understanding of transformative technologies. Among these, Artificial Intelligence (AI) has emerged as a catalyst for revolutionary change, reshaping the way businesses connect with their audiences. As we navigate this era of unprecedented innovation, the integration of AI into marketing strategies has become not just advantageous, but imperative.

Brief overview of the importance of AI in marketing

Artificial Intelligence, with its ability to analyze vast datasets, predict consumer behaviors, and automate complex tasks, has transcended its role as a mere technological advancement. It has become the linchpin for crafting marketing campaigns that resonate with unparalleled precision. From personalized customer experiences to data-driven decision-making, AI has unlocked avenues that were once considered beyond the realms of possibility. The importance of AI in marketing is not just about staying competitive; it's about reshaping the very fabric of how businesses engage, captivate, and convert their audiences.

The evolving landscape of AI marketing

The landscape of AI in marketing is a dynamic canvas, constantly evolving with breakthroughs in technology and innovative strategies. As algorithms become more sophisticated, Chabot's more

9

intuitive, and predictive analytics more accurate, the marketing landscape is undergoing a paradigm shift. This book aims to be your compass in this ever-changing terrain, guiding you through the latest trends, cutting-edge technologies, and proven methodologies that define the evolving landscape of AI marketing.

Purpose and goals of the book

The purpose of "Stay Profitable in AI Marketing" is clear to equip marketers, entrepreneurs, and business leaders with the knowledge and tools they need to harness the power of AI for sustained profitability. This book is not a theoretical exploration but a practical guide, offering insights into the real-world applications of AI in marketing. By the end of these pages, you will not only understand

10

the intricacies of AI marketing but also possess the skills to implement, optimize, and thrive in this exciting new era.

Our goals are ambitious yet tangible. We aim to demystify the complexities surrounding AI, empower you with actionable strategies, and instill the confidence to navigate the challenges that come with integrating AI into your marketing endeavors. "Stay Profitable in AI Marketing" is more than a book; it's your roadmap to not just survive but thrive in the AI-driven future of marketing. So, let's embark on this journey together, unlocking the limitless potential that AI holds for your marketing success.

CHAPTER 1

AI IN MARKETING

In the ever-evolving landscape of marketing, a fundamental grasp of Artificial Intelligence (AI) is paramount. This chapter delves into the core aspects of AI, unraveling its applications and showcasing its transformative power within the marketing realm.

Fundamentals of AI and its applications in marketing

Machine Learning: Machine learning, a subset of AI, is a powerhouse driving marketing innovation. It enables systems to learn and improve from experience without explicit programming. In marketing, machine learning algorithms analyze vast datasets to identify patterns and trends. This facilitates more accurate predictions of consumer behavior, personalized content recommendations, and dynamic pricing strategies. As we navigate through this chapter, we will explore how machine learning propels marketing campaigns to new heights, enhancing efficiency and effectiveness.

Natural Language Processing: Natural Language Processing (NLP) empowers machines to comprehend, interpret, and generate human-like language. In marketing, NLP plays a pivotal role in sentiment analysis, Chabot's, and content creation. It enables brands to engage with their audience in a conversational manner, providing personalized and seamless interactions. Unpacking the intricacies of NLP, this section will elucidate its significance in crafting compelling marketing messages and fostering genuine connections with consumers.

Predictive Analytics: Predictive analytics leverages historical data, statistical algorithms, and machine learning techniques to identify the likelihood of future outcomes. In marketing, this translates to predicting customer behaviors, optimizing ad placements, and anticipating market trends. By understanding the principles of predictive analytics, marketers can make data-driven decisions, ensuring campaigns are not just reactive but proactive in nature. This section will navigate the applications of predictive analytics, guiding readers on how to leverage this tool for strategic marketing success.

Case studies highlighting successful AI marketing strategies

The theoretical knowledge of AI in marketing finds its true value when applied in real-world scenarios. This section presents a series of case studies that exemplify how businesses have successfully harnessed AI to drive marketing innovation and achieve tangible results.

Personalization through Machine Learning:

Explore how e-commerce giants leverage machine learning algorithms to analyze user behavior and deliver personalized product recommendations. Understand how personalization enhances customer engagement, loyalty, and ultimately, boosts sales.

15

Chabot's Revolutionizing Customer Engagement:

Dive into case studies showcasing how companies in various industries have implemented AI-powered Chabot's to provide instant and personalized customer support. Discover the impact on customer satisfaction and operational efficiency.

Predictive Analytics in Targeted Marketing:

Examine instances where predictive analytics has been instrumental in identifying high-value customer segments, optimizing ad spend, and improving campaign ROI. Learn how businesses can stay ahead of the competition by anticipating market trends.

CHAPTER 2

BUILDING A SOLID FOUNDATION

As we embark on the journey to stay profitable in AI marketing, it's essential to lay a solid foundation. This chapter navigates through the critical steps of assessing your current marketing strategy, pinpointing key areas for AI integration, and setting realistic goals and expectations.

Assessing your current marketing strategy

Before venturing into the realm of AI, it is imperative to understand where your current marketing strategy stands. This involves a comprehensive evaluation of your existing processes, technologies,

17

and performance metrics. By scrutinizing your strengths, weaknesses, opportunities, and threats (SWOT analysis), you gain a holistic view of your marketing landscape. This section guides you through the assessment process, providing a roadmap to identify areas of improvement and innovation.

Identifying key areas for AI integration

Not every facet of your marketing strategy requires an AI overhaul. Strategic integration is key. This section explores how to identify the specific areas within your marketing funnel where AI can yield the greatest impact. From customer segmentation and targeting to content personalization and predictive analytics, understanding the nuanced entry points for AI ensures a targeted and effective integration. Case studies and real-

18

world examples will illuminate the successful incorporation of AI in diverse marketing scenarios.

Setting realistic goals and expectations

While the potential of AI in marketing is vast, setting realistic goals is crucial for sustainable success. This section delves into the process of aligning your AI endeavors with achievable objectives. Whether it's improving customer engagement, increasing conversion rates, or optimizing advertising spend, clarity in goal-setting ensures a focused and measurable approach. By establishing realistic expectations, marketers can avoid common pitfalls and build a foundation for long-term profitability.

CHAPTER 3

IMPLEMENTING AI TOOLS AND TECHNOLOGIES

In the quest to "Stay Profitable in AI Marketing," it's essential to not only understand the potential of AI but also to implement the right tools and technologies seamlessly. This chapter provides an insightful overview of popular AI marketing tools and strategies for their integration into existing marketing systems.

Overview of popular AI marketing tools

Chabot's and Virtual Assistants: Chabot's and virtual assistants have become integral components of AI-driven customer interactions. This section delves into the functionalities of Chabot's, exploring their use in automating customer service, facilitating e-commerce transactions, and enhancing user engagement. Virtual assistants, powered by AI, not only respond to queries but also adapt and learn from user interactions. Real-world examples and case studies demonstrate the impact of these tools in improving customer satisfaction and operational efficiency.

Personalization Algorithms: Personalization lies at the heart of effective marketing, and AI-driven personalization algorithms take this to new heights. This section explores how these algorithms analyze user data to deliver highly tailored content, product recommendations,

21

and marketing messages. Whether it's creating dynamic website experiences or crafting personalized email campaigns, personalization algorithms enhance customer engagement and foster brand loyalty.

Predictive Analytics Platforms: Predictive analytics is a game-changer in forecasting future trends and behaviors. This section provides an in-depth look at platforms that leverage AI for predictive analytics, helping marketers anticipate customer needs, optimize advertising spend, and make data-driven decisions. Case studies illustrate how businesses use predictive analytics to stay ahead of the competition and capitalize on emerging opportunities.

Integrating AI seamlessly into existing marketing systems

While adopting AI tools is crucial, the challenge lies in integrating them seamlessly into your existing marketing ecosystem. This section offers practical guidance on ensuring a smooth and effective integration process:

Audit Your Existing Systems: Conduct a comprehensive audit of your current marketing systems to identify potential points of integration. Assess compatibility, data flows, and potential areas for improvement.

Training and Onboarding: Equip your team with the necessary skills to harness AI tools effectively. This may involve training programs, workshops, or collaborating with experts to ensure a smooth onboarding process.

APIs and Integration Platforms:
Leverage Application Programming Interfaces (APIs) and integration platforms to connect AI tools with your existing marketing systems. This ensures data synchronization and seamless communication between different components of your marketing infrastructure.

Scalability and Flexibility:
Choose AI tools that are scalable and flexible, capable of growing with your business. This ensures that your marketing systems can adapt to evolving needs and technological advancements.

24

CHAPTER 4

DATA-DRIVEN DECISION MAKING

In the pursuit to "Stay Profitable in AI Marketing," data takes center stage as a key driver for informed decision-making. This chapter navigates the intricate landscape of data in AI marketing, outlining the critical role it plays, strategies for collecting and analyzing relevant data, and the paramount importance of ensuring data privacy and compliance.

The role of data in AI marketing

Data is the lifeblood of AI marketing, providing the raw material for algorithms to learn, analyze, and generate insights. This section elucidates the pivotal role that data plays in shaping effective marketing strategies powered by AI. From customer preferences and behaviors to market trends and competitive analysis, the breadth and depth of data impact every facet of AI marketing. Understanding the symbiotic relationship between AI and data is foundational to harnessing the full potential of both.

Collecting and analyzing relevant data for effective decision-making

Identifying Key Metrics: Define the key performance indicators (KPIs) that align with your marketing goals. Whether its customer engagement, conversion rates, or revenue growth, selecting relevant metrics ensures that your data collection efforts are purposeful and focused.

26

Utilizing Advanced Analytics: Beyond basic data collection, leverage advanced analytics techniques to derive meaningful insights. Machine learning algorithms can uncover patterns and trends that may not be apparent through traditional analysis, enabling more accurate predictions and strategic decision-making.

Real-time Data Monitoring: Embrace the power of real-time data monitoring to stay agile in your decision-making process. This involves continuously tracking and analyzing data as it flows in, allowing for timely adjustments to marketing strategies based on changing trends or customer behaviors.

Ensuring data privacy and compliance

Data Privacy Best Practices: Implement robust data privacy

27

measures to safeguard customer information. This section explores best practices such as data anonymization, encryption, and secure storage to protect sensitive data and build trust with your audience.

Compliance with Regulations: Navigate the complex landscape of data regulations, ensuring that your AI marketing practices align with global and regional data protection laws. From GDPR to CCPA, compliance is not just a legal requirement but a crucial aspect of maintaining ethical standards and customer trust.

Transparent Communication: Transparently communicate your data practices to your audience. Clearly articulate how data is collected, used, and protected. Establishing transparency fosters

trust and positions your brand as one that prioritizes ethical data handling.

CHAPTER 5

CREATING PERSONALIZED CUSTOMER EXPERIENCEs

In the ever-evolving landscape of marketing, the ability to deliver personalized customer experiences has become a defining factor for success. This chapter explores how Artificial Intelligence (AI) becomes the cornerstone for crafting bespoke interactions, leveraging AI for customer segmentation, customizing marketing messages and content, and enhancing the entire customer journey through personalized experiences.

Leveraging AI for customer segmentation

Dynamic Customer Segmentation: AI transcends static customer segmentation by dynamically analyzing data in real-time. This section delves into how AI algorithms identify patterns and behaviors, allowing marketers to create more nuanced and responsive customer segments. By understanding the diverse needs and preferences of individual segments, businesses can tailor their strategies for maximum impact.

Predictive Segmentation: Explore the power of predictive analytics in anticipating shifts in customer behavior. AI-driven predictive segmentation enables marketers to proactively adjust their approaches, ensuring that campaigns resonate with customers at every stage of their journey.

Customizing marketing messages and content

Personalization Algorithms in Action: This section unravels the intricacies of personalization algorithms, showcasing how they analyze user data to tailor marketing messages and content. From personalized product recommendations to individualized email campaigns, AI empowers marketers to create content that resonates on a personal level, fostering stronger connections with their audience.

Behavioral Triggers and Dynamic Content: Dive into the realm of behavioral triggers, where AI identifies customer actions and triggers automated responses. Learn how dynamic content creation

32

adapts in real-time, ensuring that the right message reaches the right audience at the right moment. This dynamic approach enhances engagement and responsiveness.

Enhancing customer journey through AI-driven personalization

Personalized Touchpoints: Explore how AI transforms touchpoints throughout the customer journey. From the first interaction to post-purchase engagement, personalized experiences create a seamless and memorable journey for customers. Case studies will illustrate how leading brands utilize AI to create cohesive and personalized customer journeys.

Cross-channel Consistency: Achieve consistency in personalized experiences across various channels. Whether customers interact through your website, mobile app, or social media, AI ensures that the personalized touch remains consistent, reinforcing brand identity and customer loyalty.

Adapting in Real-time: AI-driven personalization isn't static; it adapts in real-time based on evolving customer preferences. Discover how machine learning algorithms continuously learn from customer interactions, refining personalization strategies to meet changing expectations and market dynamics.

CHAPTER 6

OVERCOMING CHALLENGES

In the dynamic landscape of AI marketing, the journey to "Stay Profitable" is not without its challenges. This chapter addresses common obstacles in implementing AI, strategies for overcoming resistance and skepticism, and the imperative task of navigating ethical considerations in the application of AI in marketing.

Common obstacles in implementing AI in marketing

Resource Constraints: Explore how resource limitations, including budget constraints and skill shortages, pose challenges to the seamless integration of AI in marketing. Strategies for optimizing resources and identifying cost-effective solutions will be discussed.

Data Quality and Accessibility: Delve into the issues surrounding data quality and accessibility. Understand how the lack of clean, relevant data can impede the effectiveness of AI algorithms. This section offers insights into data hygiene practices and methods to enhance data accessibility.

Resistance to Change: Uncover the human aspect of resistance to change within marketing teams. Learn how to address concerns, foster a culture of adaptability, and garner support for the integration of AI technologies.

36

Strategies for overcoming resistance and skepticism

Education and Training: Discuss the importance of educating teams about the benefits and functionalities of AI. Training programs and workshops can demystify AI, alleviating skepticism and empowering teams to embrace the transformative potential of these technologies.

Transparent Communication: Emphasize the significance of transparent communication throughout the implementation process. Address concerns openly, provide clear explanations of AI functionalities, and demonstrate how these technologies complement human efforts rather than replace them.

Pilot Programs and Incremental Adoption: Propose the use of pilot programs and incremental adoption strategies. By showcasing small-scale successes and gradual integration, organizations can build confidence and trust in AI, dispelling skepticism and encouraging broader adoption.

Navigating ethical considerations in AI marketing

Consumer Privacy and Consent: Examine the ethical implications of data usage and the importance of obtaining informed consent. Explore strategies for transparently communicating data practices to consumers, building trust, and maintaining ethical standards in AI-driven marketing.

Algorithmic Bias and Fairness: Address the challenge of algorithmic bias, emphasizing the importance of fair and unbiased AI applications. This section explores methods to identify and mitigate bias in algorithms, ensuring equitable outcomes and avoiding unintended consequences.

Compliance with Regulations: Navigate the evolving landscape of data protection and AI ethics regulations. Discuss the necessity of aligning AI marketing practices with global and regional standards, reinforcing ethical considerations through compliance with legal frameworks.

CHAPTER 7

MEASURING ROI AND PERFORMANCE

In the pursuit of "Stay Profitable in AI Marketing," the ability to measure Return on Investment (ROI) and performance is paramount. This chapter outlines the crucial steps of establishing key performance indicators (KPIs) for AI marketing, analyzing the impact of AI on ROI, and the ongoing process of continuous monitoring and optimization.

Establishing key performance indicators (KPIs) for AI marketing

Defining Clear Objectives: Begin by establishing clear objectives for your AI marketing initiatives. Whether it's improving customer engagement, increasing conversion rates, or enhancing brand awareness, articulate KPIs that align with your overarching business goals.

Selecting Relevant Metrics: Explore the diverse range of metrics that can be leveraged to measure AI marketing performance. From customer acquisition cost to customer lifetime value, identify metrics that provide actionable insights into the effectiveness of your AI-driven strategies.

Aligning KPIs with Customer Journey: Tailor your KPIs to different stages of the customer journey. Understand how AI impacts customer interactions at each touchpoint and align KPIs accordingly. This ensures a comprehensive view of the customer

41

experience and the contribution of AI across the entire marketing funnel.

Analyzing the impact of AI on ROI

Attribution Modeling: Unpack the complexities of attribution modeling in the context of AI marketing. Explore how AI contributes to customer conversions and understand the various attribution models that can be employed to measure the impact on ROI.

Comparative Analysis: Conduct comparative analyses between AI-driven and traditional marketing approaches. This section provides insights into assessing the incremental benefits brought about by AI, helping marketers understand the specific contributions of these technologies to overall ROI.

Customer Segmentation Analysis: Leverage AI to analyze the impact of personalized experiences on different customer segments. Understand how AI-driven personalization influences customer behavior and contributes to increase ROI across varied target audiences.

Continuous monitoring and optimization

Real-time Analytics: Emphasize the importance of real-time analytics in the context of AI marketing. Continuous monitoring allows marketers to identify trends, track performance, and make timely adjustments to strategies, ensuring agility in response to evolving market dynamics.

A/B Testing and Iterative Optimization: Introduce the concept of A/B testing to refine AI-driven campaigns. This iterative

43

optimization process involves experimenting with different variables to identify the most effective strategies, fostering continuous improvement and adaptation.

Feedback Loops and Machine Learning Integration: Establish feedback loops that integrate machine learning insights into ongoing campaigns. Explore how the iterative learning capabilities of AI can be harnessed to refine and optimize marketing strategies over time.

44

CHAPTER 8

FUTURE TRENDS IN AI MARKETING

As we strive to "Stay Profitable in AI Marketing," a forward-looking perspective is essential to anticipate and adapt to emerging trends. This chapter explores the exciting frontier of future trends in AI marketing, encompassing the impact of emerging technologies, strategies to stay ahead of the curve, and the transformative role of AI in shaping the future of marketing.

Emerging technologies and their potential impact

Augmented Reality (AR) and Virtual Reality (VR): Delve into the potential impact of AR and VR on marketing. Explore how these immersive technologies can revolutionize customer experiences, from virtual try-ons for e-commerce to interactive brand experiences in physical spaces.

Voice Search and Conversational AI: Uncover the growing significance of voice search and conversational AI. Understand how optimizing for voice-activated search and implementing Chabot's can enhance customer interactions and reshape the way consumers engage with brands.

AI-powered Visual Recognition: Explore the potential of AI in visual recognition, allowing marketers to analyze images and videos for content moderation, brand recognition, and personalized content delivery. This section discusses the transformative impact on content marketing and user engagement.

Staying ahead of the curve in the dynamic AI landscape

Continuous Learning and Skill Development: Emphasize the importance of continuous learning in the rapidly evolving field of AI marketing. Discuss strategies for staying informed about emerging technologies, attending industry conferences, and engaging in professional development to remain at the forefront.

Agile Implementation and Experimentation: Advocate for an agile approach to implementation, encouraging marketers to experiment with new AI technologies. This section explores the benefits of iterative testing, learning from failures, and adapting strategies swiftly to capitalize on emerging opportunities.

Collaboration and Partnerships: Discuss the value of collaboration and partnerships in navigating the dynamic AI landscape. By fostering relationships with AI experts, technology providers, and industry peers, marketers can access valuable insights and stay informed about the latest developments.

The role of AI in shaping the future of marketing

Hyper-personalization and Predictive Experiences: Explore how AI will play a pivotal role in hyper-personalization, predicting customer needs before they are expressed. Discuss the implications for creating seamless and anticipatory customer experiences that drive loyalty and satisfaction.

48

AI-driven Creativity: Discuss the evolution of AI from data analysis to creative ideation. Explore how AI-generated content, design, and storytelling can complement human creativity, leading to the development of more engaging and impactful marketing campaigns.

AI in Marketing Strategy and Decision making: Examine how AI will become an integral part of marketing strategy and decision-making processes. From dynamic pricing models to strategic planning, AI's analytical capabilities will be central to shaping and optimizing overall marketing strategies.

CHAPTER 9

CONCLUSION

As we conclude our journey in "Stay Profitable in AI Marketing," it is essential to reflect on the key takeaways, emphasize the importance of ongoing learning and adaptation, and inspire readers to embrace AI for sustainable profitability in the dynamic realm of marketing innovation.

Summarizing key takeaways

AI as a Transformative Force: Recap the transformative power of AI in reshaping marketing strategies. From personalized customer experiences to data-driven decision-making, AI has emerged as a catalyst for innovation and efficiency.

Integration of AI Tools: Highlight the significance of integrating popular AI marketing tools, such as Chabot's, personalization algorithms, and predictive analytics platforms. These tools, when seamlessly incorporated, amplify marketing capabilities and contribute to improve ROI.

Data-driven Decision Making: Reinforce the importance of data-driven decision-making in the AI marketing landscape. The role of data in shaping strategies, personalizing content, and enhancing the customer journey cannot be overstated.

Overcoming Challenges: Acknowledge the challenges in implementing AI marketing, from resource constraints to resistance to change. **Emphasize the strategies outlined to overcome these obstacles and ensure a successful integration of AI technologies.**

Continuous Monitoring and Optimization: Remind readers of the continuous nature of monitoring and optimization. In the fast-paced world of AI marketing, the ability to adapt and refine strategies based on real-time insights is a key determinant of success.

Encouraging ongoing learning and adaptation

Dynamic Nature of AI Marketing: Stress the dynamic nature of AI marketing and the need for continuous learning. Encourage readers to stay informed about emerging technologies, industry trends, and evolving best practices.

Skill Development and Training: Advocate for ongoing skill development and training. The landscape of AI marketing will evolve, and marketers need to adapt by acquiring new skills, staying updated on technological advancements, and enhancing their understanding of AI applications.

Experimentation and Innovation: Inspire a culture of experimentation and innovation. Encourage marketers to embrace a mindset of trying new approaches, experimenting with AI tools, and learning from both successes and failures.

Inspiring readers to embrace AI for sustainable profitability in marketing

Embracing AI as a Strategic Asset: Conclude by emphasizing that AI is not just a technology but a strategic asset. It is a tool that, when wielded effectively, can contribute significantly to sustainable profitability in marketing.

Fostering a Proactive Approach: Inspire a proactive approach to AI adoption. Rather than waiting for industry norms to solidify, encourage readers to be pioneers in leveraging AI for marketing, gaining a competitive edge.

Building Long-term Relationships: Remind readers that AI, when harnessed ethically and strategically, is not just a means to an end but a tool for building lasting relationships with customers. Sustainable profitability is rooted in customer trust, and AI can enhance that trust through personalized and meaningful interactions.

54

As we close this chapter and the book, "Stay Profitable in AI Marketing," the journey towards sustainable profitability through AI is not just a conclusion but a commencement. The future of marketing is dynamic, and those who embrace AI with curiosity, adaptability, and strategic vision will not only stay profitable but lead the way in shaping the future of marketing innovation.

OTHER BOOKS BY THE AUTHOR
https://www.amazon.com/author/henryeparkins

Note Page

5...........................Date................

Use this page for all writing during reading or study.

Note Page
5...........................Date................

Use this page for all writing during reading or study.

Note Page
5..........................Date................

Use this page for all writing during reading or study.

Note Page
5...........................Date................

Use this page for all writing during reading or study.

Note Page
5..........................Date................

Use this page for all writing during reading or study.

Note Page
5..........................Date................

Use this page for all writing during reading or study.

Note Page
5..........................Date................

Use this page for all writing during reading or study.

Note Page
5..........................Date................

Use this page for all writing during reading or study.

Note Page
5..........................Date................

Use this page for all writing during reading or study.

Note Page
5..........................Date...............

Use this page for all writing during reading or study.

Note Page
5...........................Date................

Use this page for all writing during reading or study.

Note Page
5...........................Date................

Use this page for all writing during reading or study.

Note Page
5..........................Date................

Use this page for all writing during reading or study.

Note Page
5..........................Date................

Use this page for all writing during reading or study.

Note Page
5...........................Date................

Use this page for all writing during reading or study.

Note Page
5..........................Date.................

Use this page for all writing during reading or study.

Note Page
5..........................Date................

Use this page for all writing during reading or study.

Note Page
5...........................Date................

Use this page for all writing during reading or study.

Note Page
5..........................Date................

Use this page for all writing during reading or study.